Why I Live in
GEORGIA

101 Dang Good Reasons

Ellen Patrick

ISBN 1-58173-292-9

This book was compiled with help from Ricky &
Muriel.

Jacket and text design by Miles G. Parsons
Printed in Italy

www.booksamillion.com

1. We're what you see in the dictionary when you look up "peachy."

2. Living proof there really is a golf heaven.

3. We got everything New York has, just nicer.

4. More songs written about Georgia than any other state.

—⁓—

5. Creative use of grammar is considered an art form.

6. Suthun' Fried Chicken.

—∞—

7. Even the Devil has vacationed here.

8. Home of Jimmy.

—◊—

9. Beats living in Alabama.

10. It's illegal to eat chicken with a fork (a real ordinance in Gainesville, Georgia).

11. Live oaks.

—⁓—

12. Azaleas in spring.

13. Bass fishing so good it is sometimes mistaken for The Rapture.

14. If it was good enough for Blackbeard, it's good enough for me.

15. We gave the world Coca-Cola.

—⚬—

16. We'll grill anything.

17. We'll carpet anything.

—⁓—

18. Sherman burnt us down, but he didn't take us out.

19. State troopers will ask how your mama's doing before giving a ticket.

20. Where else can the whole family join in a seed-spittin' contest?

21. Cobbler is the #1 cure-all.

—⁂—

22. Athens, Georgia, is convenient source of world cultural trends.

23. Whitewater rafting on the Chattooga.

24. People in movies frequently pretend to be from here.

—⁐—

25. People everywhere secretly wish they were from here.

26. The lighthouse on St. Simons Island.

—⁂—

27. The Savannah riverfront.

28. Collard greens.

—∞—

29. Mustard greens.

—∞—

30. Turnip greens.

31. Georgia home cookin': widely imitated, never matched.

32. The Georgia accent: widely imitated, never matched.

33. Uga.

34. Barbecue capital of the universe.

35. No fruitcake goes uneaten.

—⁓—

36. No insult goes unpunished.

37. No chance we'll let on to Yankee tourists that we actually do have a clue.

38. Corn bread is considered a vegetable.

—⁂—

39. Beer is at the top of the Food Pyramid.

40. Bulldogs like to eat Gator meat.

—∞—

41. After God, football, and NASCAR, boiled peanuts are the most sacred.

42. More garden clubs per square mile than any other state.

43. Florida keeps the Yankees at a relatively safe distance.

—∞—

44. Blonde is the official state highlight.

45. We like grits on our butter.

46. Somebody's mama is always cooking.

47. There's a Billy Beer on every mantel.

—◊—

48. Rush hour doubles as a pickup truck parade.

49. Denim is the fabric du jour.

—◁◎▷—

50. The Big Chicken rules in Marietta.

51. Vidalia onions.

—◆◆◆—

52. Vidalia onion rings.

53. Vidalia onion salad dressing.

54. Vidalia anything.

55. Sweet potato pie.

56. Home-brewed tonics fer what ails you.

57. We don't wear pants, we wear britches.

—⟩⟨—

58. The Atlanta Motor Speedway.

59. Augusta National: where golf becomes a spiritual experience.

—⊶⊷—

60. Every Saturday is National Yard Sale Day.

61. <u>Deliverance</u>. It was only a movie. But if you're not nice to us....

62. At Tech, you can major in NASCAR theory.

—◊◊◊—

63. On Atlanta freeways, you can practice NASCAR theory.

64. Rhett and Scarlett live!

—~~~—

65. Fried catfish rules!

66. Sweet tea is king.

—✺—

67. You never know what you'll catch in the Okefenokee Swamp.

68. No one has yet explored the outer limits of hairdo height.

69. "Diet" means what you eat, not what you don't.

—⁓—

70. Neighborly good deeds still performed on a regular basis.

71. Every town has a water tower so you'll always know where you are.

72. There's a lot to be made on Georgia Tech bets.

—∞—

73. All that drinkin' evens out the playing field.

74. No shirt, no service. Overalls with no shirt, good service.

75. Home of the original Georgia Cracker.

76. Spare parts conveniently available in neighboring yards.

—◆◆◆—

77. Honky tonkin' had to start somewhere.

78. Tourist dollars
from antebellum
home tours = our little
revenge on
Mr. Sherman.

79. Laughing at the west coast is more fun from the safe distance of the east coast.

80. Hotlanta.

---

81. We wrote the book on southern hospitality.

82. Flirting is still politically correct. And correct in every other way as well.

83. In Atlanta, you can catch up on your knitting during rush hour traffic.

84. The Braves WILL DO IT.

85. The Falcons soar on Sundays.

86. Deer stands are considered vacation homes.

—⌇—

87. John Rocker was traded.

88. Relaxin' with your sweetie on a front porch swing.

89. Unbuckling your belt after Sunday dinner.

—✺—

90. Foot stompin' and toe tappin'.

91. Summer humidity reduces need for expensive moisturizers.

92. Best winter-storm parties in the whole U.S. of A.

93. Mall hoppin'.

—⚬⚬—

94. Bar hoppin'.

95. Buttermilk biscuits.

—⁓—

96. Homemade jerky.

97. You can wallpaper your home with leftover lottery tickets.

98. Dogs ride shotgun; people ride in the truck bed.

99. Ted You-Know-Who.

100. Plenty of snakes in case you're in the mood for handlin'.

101. You can leave Georgia, but you'll always come back home.